Flower Power

Basil

Roxy

Based on the original Basil Brush animations
Illustrated by Bill Ledger
Story adapted by Clare Robertson

Basil was going to see Roxy.

"Roxy likes flowers," he said.
"I will give her some flowers."

"Oh no! There are no flowers in my garden," said Basil. But he had a plan.

Basil went to a garden with lots of flowers.

"This is the best flower. I will pick this one," said Basil.

But the flower did not like it.

The flower ate Basil!

Then the flower spat Basil out.

Basil was cross.
"I will be back," he said.

Basil came back with a digger.
"Now I will get that flower!
Boom! Boom!" he said.

It did not work! But Basil had a new plan to get some flowers.

Basil went into the big hall. There were lots of people inside.

Basil went on stage.
He sang a song.

The people liked
the song.

They liked it so much that they threw flowers.

One man threw a flower in a pot!

Basil took the flowers.
"Now I will go and see Roxy."
said Basil.

Basil gave Roxy the flowers.
"Thank you, Basil!" said Roxy.

VIDEO GAME REVOLUTION
THE BASICS OF GAME DESIGN

by Heather E. Schwartz

Raintree is an imprint of Capstone Global Library Limited, a company incorporated in England and Wales having its registered office at 264 Banbury Road, Oxford, OX2 7DY – Registered company number: 6695582

www.raintree.co.uk
myorders@raintree.co.uk

Text © Capstone Global Library Limited 2020
The moral rights of the proprietor have been asserted.

All rights reserved. No part of this publication may be reproduced in any form or by any means (including photocopying or storing it in any medium by electronic means and whether or not transiently or incidentally to some other use of this publication) without the written permission of the copyright owner, except in accordance with the provisions of the Copyright, Designs and Patents Act 1988 or under the terms of a licence issued by the Copyright Licensing Agency, Barnard's Inn, 86 Fetter Lane, London, EC4A 1EN (www.cla.co.uk). Applications for the copyright owner's written permission should be addressed to the publisher.

Editor: Gena Chester
Designers: Kay Fraser and Rachel Tesch
Media researcher: Tracy Cummins
Original illustrations © Capstone Global Library Limited 2020
Production Specialist: Kathy McColley
Originated by Capstone Global Library Ltd
Printed and bound in India

ISBN 978 1 4747 8806 9 (hardback)
ISBN 978 1 4747 8812 0 (paperback)

British Library Cataloguing in Publication Data
A full catalogue record for this book is available from the British Library.

Acknowledgements
We would like to thank the following for permission to reproduce photographs: Alamy: Kevin Britland, 17; Getty Images: TOSHIFUMI KITAMURA/AFP, 15; Shutterstock: Anna Chernova, Design Element, aurielaki, Cover, Christos Georghiou, Design Element, Designworkz, Design Element, Dragon Images, 27, EKKAPHAN CHIMPALEE, 21, Fotos593, 4, FrameStockFootages, 22, George W. Bailey, 7, Jacek Chabraszewski, 9, Lauren Elisabeth, 29, NuPenDekDee, 11, 13, Pedro Martinez Valera, 16, sezer66, 19, silverkblackstock, 25, VectorPixelStar, Design Element, yurakr, Design Element.

Every effort has been made to contact copyright holders of material reproduced in this book. Any omissions will be rectified in subsequent printings if notice is given to the publisher.

All the internet addresses (URLs) given in this book were valid at the time of going to press. However, due to the dynamic nature of the internet, some addresses may have changed, or sites may have changed or ceased to exist since publication. While the author and publisher regret any inconvenience this may cause readers, no responsibility for any such changes can be accepted by either the author or the publisher.

CONTENTS

CHAPTER 1
Collecting ideas 4

CHAPTER 2
Putting it on paper 10

CHAPTER 3
Getting focused 14

CHAPTER 4
Learning more 24

Glossary 30

Find out more 31

Websites 31

Index 32

COLLECTING IDEAS 1

Inspiration can come from anywhere! The book *One Thousand and One Nights* has inspired many video games, including the popular *Prince of Persia* series.

Want to be a video game designer? If you love playing video games, you're on the right track already. When you play video games, you learn more about them. This can help you create games of your own.

PAY ATTENTION LIKE A PRO

Even professional game designers play video games because it's fun. But they also pay careful attention to how games work while they're playing. You can take the same approach.

Notice how different games are played. Some have an objective. You try to win battles against opponents or reach higher levels. Others focus more on building or exploring a **virtual** world. Games also have different styles and graphic elements. All of these details come together to create different kinds of games. Which details do you like enough to include in your own design?

Ideas for video games can come from anywhere. Sometimes real-life events spark ideas. Dreams and nightmares offer ideas too. You might be inspired by a book or film that you love.

> **FACT!**
> Drawing inspiration from your favourite games is fine. But **plagiarizing** isn't. Make sure your game is original and doesn't directly copy someone else's idea.

plagiarize to copy someone else's work and pass it off as your own

virtual when a location, person or object exists only as part of a computer program

WHERE IN THE WORLD?

Early ideas eventually become a rough draft. Jot down notes and thoughts. Write a short version of the story of your game. Include the age and skill level of the people who will enjoy your game. This is called your **target audience**.

Many video games take place in a fictional world. As the game designer, you get to create it. Your world will need a setting, characters and a story line. The setting is where the game takes place. Think about what your world looks like.

Also consider its tone. Is it a happy place or a scary place? Characters are the humans, animals or other creatures living in the world you create. People who play your game will move the characters to make things happen.

Finally, the **plot** is the general goal of the game. Do your characters battle each other? Do they explore a world together? The story can be as simple or complicated as you like.

You don't have to get everything right the first time. Be prepared to revise your ideas along the way. That's how they'll get better.

In the *Legend of Zelda: Breath of the Wild*, the players control the character Link. The game's goal is for Link to save the kingdom of Hyrule from Calamity Ganon.

plot the main story of a piece of writing

target audience a particular group for whom a film, book or video game is made

BUILDING A STORY

Most stories in video games follow the same patterns found in books or films. Pay attention, and you'll see they usually follow a **story arc**. A story arc begins with background information. Players learn about the world they're in and the characters they're meeting.

Once a background has been established, players go through rising action. Here the main character faces a **conflict**. He or she makes choices that move the story forward. You reach the **climax** of the story when the conflict is at its highest point. In a game, that could be the moment a player wins or loses. After the climax, falling action shows what happens after.

The end of your plot or story is called the resolution. It doesn't have to be happy, but it should be satisfying for a player.

climax a story's most exciting moment

conflict the main issue in your story

story arc a series of events from beginning to end in a story

Get the creative juices flowing

Can't come up with ideas? Brainstorming techniques can help. Try these to get started:

- Make a list of words that describe the world you want to create.
- Draw a character you'd like to include in your game.
- Go running or cycling and brainstorm after. Exercise can make your brain think more creatively.

PUTTING IT ON PAPER 2

Have you ever tried explaining a video game to someone who hasn't played it before? It's hard! That's because video games are **visual**. People need to see them to understand what you're talking about. Explaining a game that hasn't been created yet is even more difficult.

storyboard a series of drawings that shows the story of a TV show, film or video game

visual to do with seeing

Game designers get around this problem with a very simple fix. Instead of just talking, they create a **storyboard**. A storyboard is a set of drawings that show how the game works and what happens when players reach new levels in a game.

Storyboards also help game designers work through their games. When you create your storyboard, you might find questions that need to be addressed. Or you can test out ideas that you're unsure about in the storyboard. You'll know then whether or not they'll work out.

How the pros do it

Professional storyboard artists study films to understand how the camera works to tell a story. They also study drawing so they can show characters' feelings and movements without using words. Special software helps these pros create storyboards on a computer. Programs such as StudioBinder, Moviestorm, ShotPro and StoryBoard Quick help storyboard artists showcase their creativity.

FACT!
Artists working on the film *Three Little Pigs* at Walt Disney Studios in the 1930s developed one of the first ever storyboards.

DO IT YOURSELF!

Your storyboard doesn't need to include every detail of your game. A basic outline will work. After that's done, you can add more detail if you choose.

To begin, draw six squares on a sheet of paper. These are your storyboard panels. Draw what's happening in each panel from the beginning to the end of your game. You can add more panels as you go through your game to its end. It's important to make sure your storyboard shows events in order.

If you're an amazing artist, this might be one of your favourite parts of designing a game! But don't worry if the opposite is true. Quick, basic drawings called sketches will work just as well as detailed drawings. Each picture can include a few words to explain what's happening at that point in the story.

FACT!
A Pixar animation team does more than 4,000 storyboard drawings to plan a whole film.

GETTING FOCUSED

With a storyboard on paper you can start to fine-tune. What **point of view** will you show in your game? Will players look down from the sky or get a full view from the ground? How many people will be able to play your game at once? What kind of music should you add to your game?

point of view eyes through which a story is told

FACT!
Nintendo hired its first video game music composer, Koji Kondo, in 1984.

Koji Kondo

Game designers have to look at every part of the picture. Will the main character have special powers? How many? How can players get them? Will each level of the game have a different look? Game designers need to answer each of these questions and more. That way they'll be prepared when the time comes to develop the game.

If it sounds like a lot to think about, don't stress. Game designers don't start out by creating complicated games. They start simple. A 1970s video game called *Pong* was a simplified version of table tennis. It had two lines for paddles and a circle for a ball.

THE NITTY-GRITTY

You don't need to get complicated the first time you create a game. But there's one detail you can't forget. Your game needs a name!

The title of your game could be almost anything, and there are many examples you can look to for ideas. Some titles, such as *Sonic the Hedgehog* and *Super Mario Maker*, are named after characters. Others, such as *Splatoon* and *Xenoblade Chronicles*, include made-up words.

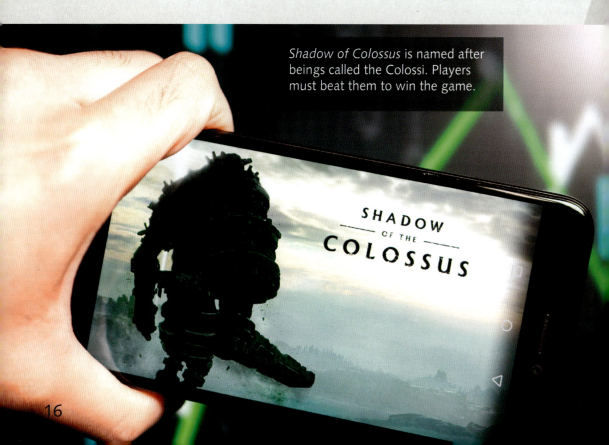

Shadow of Colossus is named after beings called the Colossi. Players must beat them to win the game.

Donkey Kong is another video game named after its main character.

List video game names that you like, and consider why you like them. Then try to think of and list names for your game.

GETTING SERIOUS 😎

You've created a storyboard. You have lists of ideas and pages of notes. Feeling disorganized? Any game designer would at this point. That's why professional game designers put all of their ideas together in what's called a Game Design Document, or GDD. A GDD is meant as a guide for all the people who will work on your game. It can be created in pages on a computer or with papers gathered together in a folder. The pages include everything about your game divided into sections.

The first section is a short description of your game. Imagine you're talking to a friend. Explain in a minute or less how the game works and why it would be fun to play. Try to keep it between 150 and 250 words.

The next section is about your target audience. Here you can describe the people you imagine playing your game. State whether these players will be children or adults and give an age range for your game. You can also talk about whether this game will challenge serious gamers or whether it will be easier to play.

FACT!
Nearly 32 million people play video games in the UK.

The GDD isn't finished yet! The next section game designers focus on is platform. This deals with how people will access your game. As a gamer, you know some games are meant for mobile devices, a game **console** or a computer.

The next section in your GDD focuses on **genre**. Just like books and films, video games fit into certain genres. Action, sports, role-playing and racing are all examples of genres. Your game might fit into one genre or a combination of two or more.

After that, you need a section titled "core game play". In this section, describe in detail how the game is played. Add more details than you did in your short description section. Here, game designers explain characters' goals and how they move, such as by running and jumping. They also include information about the controls players use to create those actions.

console a panel with dials and switches for controlling an electronic device

genre a category that contains a common theme, for example action or sports

Controls on a computer are found on the mouse or the keyboard. Console controls are on a handheld controller.

FACT!
Teamwork can be more satisfying than solo work. It causes the brain to release oxytocin, a chemical that makes people feel good.

The last two sections of your GDD are fun places to show your creativity. The visual style section is where you describe the appearance and setting of the game you have in mind. Use your writing skills to talk about when and where your game takes place and how you want your game to look.

After you've completed that, the next section covers the characters and plot. Describe the different characters' personalities and appearances. Tell the story they're moving through. You can include your storyboard in the GDD too. Then you have two chances to get your message across.

The GDD covers everything about your game and everything that needs to get done to make it real. Because of that, it's a lot of work! Pro game designers generally work with a team that includes programmers, artists and other professionals. Recruit your friends! A GDD helps you work with others to make the process easier and more enjoyable.

CRACKING THE CODE

Coding is an important piece of the puzzle for video game design. You can learn coding through Scratch, Code.org or other free programming sites. Software on these sites teaches users to build interactive stories, games and animations. When you're ready, you can move up to more advanced software programmes, such as Unity.

If you like learning on your own, there are plenty of online tutorials you can watch about coding. You can also try coding classes where you can learn with a teacher. Schools or public libraries might offer free sessions too.

Professional game designers don't have to do all the coding work. That job belongs to game programmers. However, you'll be a more successful game designer if you understand all the steps in the process.

> **code** a computer language that serves as instructions for computers

GAME DESIGN GOALS

If you want a future in gaming, consider all of its different careers. Game designers focus on stories and creative ideas for games. But you could also be a graphic artist. Graphic artists draw the art and animation. Maybe you want to be a video game composer and create the music for games. Or you might enjoy working as a game programmer, coding games to bring them to life.

For now, dream up some idea of games you'd love to play. Work on them as much as you like before moving on to your next game ideas. Keep learning about and playing video games. Who knows? Your passion for gaming could one day become a career!

FACT!
In 2018, there were 47,620 people working in the video game industry in the UK.

Bethesda Game Studios is a US video game company that's developed popular series such as *The Elder Scrolls* and *Fallout*. As of 2018, 400 people work at the company.

Glossary

climax a story's most exciting moment

code a computer language that serves as instructions for computers

conflict the main issue in your story

console a panel with dials and switches for controlling an electronic device

genre a category that contains a common theme, for example action or sports

plagiarize to copy someone else's work and pass it off as your own

plot the main story of a piece of writing

point of view eyes through which a story is told

story arc a series of events from beginning to end in a story

storyboard a series of drawings that shows the story of a TV show, film or video game

target audience a particular group for whom a film, book or video game is made

virtual when a location, person or object exists only as part of a computer program

visual to do with seeing

Find out more

Coding Games from Scratch (Code it Yourself), Rachel Ziter (Raintree, 2018)

Computer Games Designer (The Coolest Jobs on the Planet), Mark Featherstone (Raintree, 2014)

STEAM Jobs for Gamers (STEAM Jobs), Sam Rhodes (Raintree, 2018)

Video Game Trivia: What You Never Knew about Popular Games, Design Secrets and the Coolest Characters (Not Your Ordinary Trivia), Sean McCollum (Raintree, 2018)

Websites

Hour of Code
code.org/learn

Scratch
scratch.mit.edu/

Unity
unity3d.com/programming-in-unity

Index

brainstorming 9
characters 6, 7, 8, 9, 11, 15, 16, 20, 23
classes 24, 25, 26
climax 8
coding 26, 28
computer programs 11, 26
conflict 8
Game Design Document (GDD) 18, 20, 23
genres 20
graphic artist 28
graphics 5
inspirations 4, 5
objectives 5
opponents 5
plots 6, 8, 23
Pong 15
professionals 11, 18, 23, 25, 26
resolution 8
rising action 8
settings 6, 23

story arcs 8
storyboards 11, 12, 13, 14, 18, 23
story lines 6
target audience 6, 18
titles 16, 20
virtual 5
worlds 6, 8, 9, 25